THE YEAR OF NOT DANCING

THE YEAR OF NOT DANCING

C.L. Dallat

For Keto
with all best wishes

[signature]

Jackaville
8th March '17

BLACKSTAFF
PRESS

BELFAST

First published in 2009 by
Blackstaff Press
4D Weavers Court, Linfield Road
Belfast BT12 5GH
with the assistance of the Arts Council of Northern Ireland

Reprinted 2015

EPIGRAPH: 'Autumn Leaves' © 1947 Enoch Et Cie
and Ardmore Music Corp. Words and music by
Jacques Prevert and Joseph Kosma.
English translation by Johnny Mercer.
Published by Peter Maurice Music Co. Ltd
and EMI Music Publishing.

Typeset by IMD Typesetting and Design, Kent
Printed and bound by CPI Group UK (Ltd), Croydon CR0 4YY

A CIP catalogue record for this book
is available from the British Library

ISBN 978-0-85640-840-3

www.blackstaffpress.com

in memoriam
Mary Constance Dallat
(née Gilligan)

1925–1964

Since you went away
The days grow long
And soon I'll hear
Old winter's song . . .

from 'Autumn Leaves' ('Les Feuilles Mortes')
JACQUES PRÉVERT AND JOSEPH KOSMA

English lyrics by
JOHNNY MERCER

CONTENTS

For Years   1

Carrick-a-Rede Rope Bridge   3

Sentence   4

Worries on Your Doorstep   5

Notebook   6

In Paradisum   8

After Days in Blind-Drawn Rooms   9

Dance Lessons   10

Lido Café   12

County Down   13

Salvador   14

The Year of Not Dancing   15

The Last Mortician   16

Eternity Where?   18

So Many Revolutions Per Minute   19

Love on a Rock   20

Difference   22

Grandfather   24

Careless Talk   25

Hand-painted Ties   27

Lives of the Composers   28

Cyclops   30

Summer's End   31

Wrong about Love   32

Les Amants	33
Calling the Shots	35
City Love Songs	36
The New Life	38
Too Much Reality	39
Impedimenta	41
Do Not Watch the Eclipse of the Sun, My Love	42
Bedsit	43
Dandelion Clock	44
South	45
Not Buying a Dog	47
Getting Started	49
Island	51
Et in Arcadia	52
Pavlova's Dogs	53
Swooping	54
In a Cold Climate	56
African Queen	57
Out of Touch, My Baby	59
Boarding-house Bookcase	61
Noli-Me-Tangere	62
Old Winter's Song	63

FOR YEARS

Almost unbidden, more sigh
than tacit prayer in a heartfelt world,

not for one fellow homefarer
hefted chest high and still
among crash-helmeted Day-Glo bearers,
helmed holmward under red blankets
this rushing-hour rain-soft Monday to
the slightly aggrieved mumbling of two thousand turbos,

but for a someone piercing film
on vegetable tikka masala
in a new cul-de-sac on the flood plain
south-west of the reservoir
parrying persistent entreaties
between news and *EastEnders*
re-dialling a number that rings in a locked Samsonite
in admissions' one three-drawer cabinet,

or for someone on a black plastic chair
days afterward, registering death
where they'd last come, both, with good news

and for the kids alone among crowds
back at St Polycarp's in September
and for next Guy Fawkes' –

for Augusts that fail differently
from others' failed family sorties
and being unequal to speaking
for years. For forty or more years.

CARRICK-A-REDE ROPE BRIDGE

Never made it to the L-shaped land
that bulked between us and horizon,

never swayed on that defying fishery bridge
till my own were grown and fearless:

remembered then an eleven-plus-money
darkroom tank, Ilford contact prints of
my slow-stepping lean grandfather,
quivering hand on homburg at a car-door here;
by the great ruined hall above white horses; or
scratching in his ciphered diary with a sporadic
Conway Stewart, while about him whispers
in the family estate car perplexed, why
oughtn't he stay through September, which
son's house he'd visit next?
                       When he left
I started a new school and the ambulance came
for his – forty-four years younger – daughter.
Six weeks, and she'd go six months before him.

SENTENCE

Once four doors down
and again at the harbour yard
when men in dark, dark blue
with peaked caps and silvered
buttons had come to take
someone to a white van with steps,
both times I was told
this wasn't 'being arrested':
but I knew there was no plea bargain
for remission the day
the same men in uniforms
came up our staircase
and into my mother's room.

WORRIES ON YOUR DOORSTEP

From far enough off it's blindingly clear
why one of her few married portraits
– twenties and forties studio poses
had either Grimms' tales or a mortarboard –
should be over at Walshes' box-hedge
holding the younger three, Ciaran
with the bubble hoop: though in my print
they're all cropped.
              Even if my father's Dresden
Zeiss-Ikon had more stops than an Ilford,
silver salts only registered the far,
sun-blistered side.
            The furrowed look
I'd long ascribed to pre-diagnostic intuition
was mere strained squint at a blurred
noonish sun leaching out over Hospital Field,
mortuary, the convent terraces, in stifling
vehicle-less dog-hours before the auxiliary
siren would summon hosiers, dolemen,
sawmill-clerks, wainwrights, hot-foot
– casting off shopcoats, brown aprons,
fastest mustered brigade in the county –
by moped, shanks's pony, Corsair,
to their newly built voluntary fire-station.

NOTEBOOK

Thurs. p.m. took this week's
'Market Street News' up to ward. Friday
her friend drives us to Belfast, stop at
brother's (Antrim Rd), red-haired boy
plays in Wendy House, whole front-room
like play-room, then uncle's place on
Malone, kidney-shaped dressing-table,
three mirrors, stool, circular bay;
72 downtown, pick-up again
outside Newell's, Royal Ave; then
Majestic where she took us to
Danny Kaye and 'Thumbelina' six
years ago, tonight *Beach Party*, girl sings
To know, know, know him . . . in mirror.

Sat. a.m. visit to uncle's office –
drawing office – on Dublin Rd
opposite controversial bank sculptures,
Gardner's on Botanic for Penguins (still
Don Camillo), tropical ravine house,
casserole with mince, rice, carrots;
fireworks at neighbours' for Hallowe'en
plus their bonfire for 5th Nov., early,
then John's conjuring tricks for cousins
and neighbours' children. Bath and bed.

Called down late to say rosary with aunt,
uncle gone to Market St Sunday,
her friend's brother drives us home –
she's in tears. More rosaries. Outside

hospital at fuel inlet, friend's brother
talks about working by the *Telegraph*
watching ink-tankers deliver. Other
uncle back from Indiana. Talks
about my book-review index-cards
and what I want to be in the end. Not sure;
I still think reporter. No 'Market Street
News' scheduled next week.

IN PARADISUM

A rare winter sun cuts
through the late afternoon:
Davy, who'd worked
forty-odd years with
my grandfather and his
orange-growing son,
hand-holds our three sisters
by the new station wagon

       as we step

from mortuary chapel
amid quiet flow of cousins,
uncles, the new priest
who sang 'Scarlet Ribbons'
last snowfall, and a whole,
death-silenced town.

AFTER DAYS IN BLIND-DRAWN ROOMS

Odd, a grown-up speaking to you in the street,
like you were a real person, the enveloped card
in the empty wicker basket and you knew
what it looked like without seeing, with dozens
at home, masses, perpetual offerings, but she
met you at Archie McKinley's and turned
and stepped along with you, and talked down the road
past Molloy's with the sixteen big windows, past
the fire-station, by Blackmore's coal and the market-yard
– weighbridges, threshers, Lister twine-balers –
and you said you were due up at the Legion of Mary
but this was the first anyone said they knew what you felt,

and by the foot of the hill you were doing the *Cantata*,
bright as the sun and *terrible as an army* and
my soul doth magnify . . . verse and response, like a
two-handed routine, and then you could see her,
instead of somebody's mum in a seafront
dormer-roofed house, aproned and calling
and making and sending, you saw her a girl
in a belted coat in a grey, blind-drawn house
one March Friday evening between two wars,
missing her own Legion meeting in some painted chapel,
kneeling at home by the brother who died,
a brother she'd never stopped thinking of since but
hadn't had much cause to mention, no need until now.

DANCE LESSONS

Twice a year the priest can
say three masses end-to-end:
the last time for All Souls
including, that day, my mother,
this time for Christmas midnight,
though Father Lynch – who saluted
the staircase rodent – lost his place
in the second at *Orate, fratres!*
shaking his hoary locks and
repeating from *Sursum corda.*
I missed the *Hanc igitur* bell,
catching up at *Hoc est enim,*
meaning *Emmanuel* was *with us*
four times that cloudless night.

For altar-boy tact – not openly
mocking the Lord's anointed –
our reward was an ice-rink hill
we slalomed down, belting *Adeste . . .*
to the bus-stop and public toilets
in front of the Anzac Bar.
By day we staged a snow-blitz
for the cameraman up our road
and – after the Queen's speech
and trimmings at Aunt Kate's –
watched ourselves on UTV
being pushed aside by boys
from Star-of-the-Sea. Daily,
till term began, we were asked
to someone's for tea (with chips),

including those second cousins
– teenagers with fringes and EPs –
who taught us the Mashed Potato
in their parlour above the barber's
to *Help me information,*
more than that I cannot add.

LIDO CAFÉ

First he taught us to step off
the back of a moving CIÉ bus,
run a few steps to absorb
momentum before turning back,
like he'd done on the Crumlin Road
in his theology student days;
then how to sprinkle vinegar
down into the paper cone
– even if it wasn't a *Telegraph* –
before dredging with salt, lightly
juggling heat; first time we'd
seen a plastic tomato of ketchup
or smoked-glass coffee cups,
first time we'd been out in a café
together, the girls asleep in Mrs
McKee's on the Clontarf Road,
his brother and sister coming
down next day to help out with
the seven of us, but tonight just
John, me and him on a CIÉ bus.

COUNTY DOWN

That dead day we whirled without end
through a solemnity of small hills,
inspected the placid asylum, distillery –
my grandfather's ruin – bypassed
masonic obsequies on the front,
snaked under glowering scarps
to the farm of my once-removed –
source of our one personalised
season's greeting – and peered
over narrow black waters to another country,
to the *Arsenic-&-Lace* forest lodge
where no one served breakfast, where we'd stood
by our eldest uncle with a Volkswagen,
guidebook and daughters, the summer after.

SALVADOR

The stuntman who was Dali's Christ
is dead then, in today's *Guardian*,
who looked down sheer from the cross-piece
through blood-veiled eyes past biceps
and coach-bolted metatarsals on a waterworld
of pearl-fisher sculls, looked down
from the uncles'-room wallpaper
(on the bed where I'd last seen Granda)
that over-easy August morning
when John and I woke in the second
week of our da's second honeymoon
and Frankie came round with a bottle
of raspberryade and a king-size bag
of prawn-flavour crisps to head out
to the school for Junior results after
we'd gone to the side-chapel to pray.

THE YEAR OF NOT DANCING

Hours passed languid as the flap of a hawk's wing
in a last July before the awkward initiations
of fifteen and lifts to far-afield jiving.

He'd work for an uncle, cutting hay, fixing
shingles with bradawls and hot, smoking pitch –
evenings, hung round with fairground hands

till the sideshows lit at eight. Then he'd sidestroke
from the main pier, alone, on a full tide as far
as the bobbing *Perpetua*, its line of cork floats,

with dock and fairground small as a snow-bubble town,
bullhorns carrying Frank Ifield's *When the angels ask
me to recall* out across a calm, irredentist blackness.

THE LAST MORTICIAN

Who would there be to see to
my undertaker uncle
                    dying the day
between his two saints' feasts, one
for country, the other for a calling
he'd follow his father Peter the fiddler
into, a franchise we'd had since
the Whitehill branch got their first
long-wheelbase cart before Emancipation?

It would fall to my father, ten years
schoolmastering away from the trade,
twenty since he'd left Patrick's band –
the older brother's wide, rich trumpet
a pre-TB legend half the country'd fox-
trotted loves-of-their-lives to, 'Stardust',
'Body and Soul', conceding post-war
to the alto sax my father then abandoned,
dreading coughed blood, to the nimble
clarinet he'd gliss till declining a last
Blue Angels gig the night I was born.

And had we a shared thought
- two brothers, two bereft cousins -
on a breezeblock wall watching him
silent in shirtsleeves, braces,
coffin-house double-doors wide that
big cold spring morning, lining a quality
model his brother'd shellacked?

No 'Am I
my brother's – ?'
                No thought, as he'd
gather-tension-fire with the staple-gun,
gather, tension, fire again, that we'd
witnessed Patrick follow the same
rubric a balmy November day
three years before with sky-blue silk.

Only that what my father turned his hand to
he'd make a job of, as his new wife called us
to our own yard to take him tea and
her sugared, crumbling shortbread.

ETERNITY WHERE?

When those weathery captains-emeritus
of southern sea-roads, in generations
after the early conquistadors, finally
hung braided topcoats and spyglasses
and repaired to *estancias* their *pour-cent*
of iron-pyrites had earned them,

they'd annex one *stanza* at the shade-end
of the meridian cloister, have it painted
all-round aquamarine to eyeball-height
of one seated at compass and charts
and sky-blue thereabove, their balm for
nostalgia: the ache for our own things . . .

On my part – for my share of the world –
the eye-line'll be lower: I'm becalmed
on a Ford Zephyr estate's blue-greyish
rear seat on a cold Congregational
Sabbath seafrontage; below,
unflinching pewter of squalls
between pierhead and headland and island;
above – unremitting – slate-grey.

SO MANY REVOLUTIONS PER MINUTE

Ira didn't want to set the world
on fire, circumnavigated, started
revolutions in Spain, *the living
is easy*, he'd write, Remington-ing
the text to brother George's
'Summertime', but somebody'd
started a blaze in the barracks
on the eleventh evening.

'IRA', on the other hand, flared
briefly (hindsight requires
'old' or 'bracket-fifty-seven-
close-bracket'), etched in black
on the main square's pavement-high
wine-cellar windowsills
on the downhill to gasworks
and farrier's shop, or Biro'd
on calloused knuckles of a boy
from the head of the town, who,
on the other hand, eight years
after, *étonné*'d the *immigré*
singing-*meister* at the convent;
momentarily time-shifted
by felt-tipped back-of-the-hand
Aryan symbols, his Flemish
eyebrows raised as mine are this first
Rajasthan dawn in a hi-tech sector,
watching from a glass lift, some
wars later, a crocodile of blazer-and-
badged senior infants file through
wrought gates to Swastika Junior.

LOVE ON A ROCK

Who could tell them now – out in the world,
its plethorae of arc-lights, halogens, discos –
those lighthouse children with listening eyes,
now the last tin cup, plate and fork
are stowed in the last canvas bag under
a fo'c'sle and rowed with their owner
to the supply port, gold watch and severance.

But you'd know them then in utility brown-
and-cream rooms, wiser in their generations
than world-children; at jonquil Formica tables,
sucked HB stubs at poise to take down
wireless PO boxes, or describe collections
and hobbies to comics; devouring a quarter's worth –
in a morning – of *Dandy*s and *Beano*s and *Judy*s
since the weather last faired; or dwelling
on all missing lightkeeping men . . .
know them playing ecksy-oseys in winter,
hopscotching the one slab of cement
between storm door and fairweather jetty:
and know by their manners when bible-people
came with flasks in baskets and Old Testament
crayoning books, or hikers with tripods
to put the rock in their textbooks and maps.

You might see them still, if you're careful
on city-hall or tower-block stairways, left
foot tiptoed on an absent stiletto from years
navigating anti-clockwise tight spiral stairs:
or find them when everyone's gone,

rocking against the emulsioned wall
in the dark of a seventh-floor office
and the sound that you hear isn't them
but the thinness of baby seals' weeping
or the contralto with auburn-grey wisps
chanting the *bright stormy sea* as she folds
the cold grey sheet down and Trinity-
House-issue blankets, tells them never
to fret. Or their lilting along to the small-
gansied man with pipe-grime under
his left index nail rippling a hornpipe's
slow triplets on a Breton concertina.

And you'll know them in truth for children
of the rocks, for they'll have preset
the Xerox's counter right up to the thousand,
lid-up and nothing on the glass, eyelids
numb on the margin of sleep as the phasings
of light take them home to the beam-room again.

DIFFERENCE

Crawford Ballantyne had a bugle.
Collected car numbers. *It's just*
something you do. But when
I bought a 3D Silvine, he offered
to report me to the barracks.
His da, Tommy, caught me
caught on a gravel bank below
the stone bridge in Reserved Waters.
Swore at me for poaching.
You . . . But he didn't say what.

His people were more into
traditional dance-tunes than ours.
All those full sets of pipes
stored now like contraband in attics
of quiet farm-buildings: at least
with a flute you could keep your hand in.
Crawford had no time for guitars
- *Have some respect for your culture* –
but no emphasis on the *your.*
More like our sort than ourselves.

Only twice did the differences out.
Striding uphill to the chapel
to help the injured: *I knew*
this would happen, shooting me
one of those looks. Or maybe:
I knew this was going to happen.
And then at one of our funerals,
he took second last lift of the coffin

right to the gates and then neatly
stepped aside. But it counted. That twice
was more or less the extent of it.

GRANDFATHER

Sat on a dining-room chair he had turned
himself years before, he'd sip tea as I played,
bounded by back doorstep and pram,
the meat safe where butter cooled under a muslin
with ends dipped in water, a hopper with suds
guttering out of our single-tub washing machine.

Once, perhaps high with hopes, perhaps
with a notion he hadn't long left, we set out
past limehouse and locked coffin-shop up to
the orange groves Patrick planted in the war:
cutting a hazel wishbone,
he planted his chair and sat down.

He'd have known the run of the burn
from Hospital Field through the culvert,
but I walked up and down for what seemed like ages.
All he would say: *You're as bad as your da.*
Then: *One last go.* But this time he gripped
my arms at the elbow and this time it leapt.

Grown, I walked the same stretch with my da,
asked if he knew there was water below
and he told me how Granda once took him
that same hopeful trip at seven or eight:
and did it twitch? *No! Well, maybe just once –
when he gave up and took my wrists in his hands.*

CARELESS TALK

Sheds were made from something other then;
wooden uprights crumbling in your hand,
fastened with spiderweb and spores –
wall-boards layered with tarry felt.

                         Tom
over-the-road battled with Fablon, carpet,
onion-box slats, to keep his bantams
from traffic.

            The one next door we illuminated
with stolen altar candles till it, too, lit.

                     Ours
was linked to a recent war – not just
the mushroom years but secrets it still held:
ladies' bicycles we'd regret my father
painting beige-and-white (others our age
raced head-down while we pedalled
streets like William Trevor spinsters,
high handlebars and baskets without jam);
a trunk (no bodies, we checked), lined
with our sitting-room's embossed paper;
glass-topped, three-foot-high cabinet, black,
with lampholder and high-watt, silvered lamp,
a prototype copier bought army-surplus
to languish toner-less in this bunker
without power, for reasons we couldn't divine;
gas-masks still in wartime shop-bought boxes
we could have used for plays or fancy-dress
except

            all talk in the house implied this shed
didn't exist, a convention we observed

until Chris's dad came round one May night
to ask, before they packed for Montreal,
how much my father wanted for a trunk
of whose existence no one knew, officially.

HAND-PAINTED TIES

Direct from one of those damp
West Yorkshire wool-cities
with just one tied suitcase,
he stood the length of a Fair Day
at the Seaham Arms lamp post,
a distant-something of one of Sikorski's
airmen from the resettlement homes,
right arm signpost-rigid,
decked tip-to-shoulder with what seemed
– in clothes-coupon years – a gross
of hand-painted ties, left hand
repeatedly un- and re-folding
the wad in a right-inside pocket,
and went back to own a string
of horses.
        Yet now, thinking on,
it wasn't habanera swirls,
chrome yellows and parakeet greens,
but fedora, box-back suit, signet
– maybe implied cornet or Dillinger –
we thought we could buy
for thirteen-and-six, a ransom,
that heady apples-and-toffee day
in the wake of a war that was surely
none of our making, way up here.

LIVES OF THE COMPOSERS

Partly the Doric flourish, soda-bar chrome
of the Rock-Ola in Joe's Carousel pavilion –
partly the gunmetal changer that actioned
the selection, A-nineteen or J-eight,
volunteering a line-up suspect
to press into drill on the deck
click
    then revolution after revolution
the names: Schroeder,
swirling with Resnick, Spector, Vogel.
Holly, Petty, Hardin were the Crickets,
then, ceaselessly, Lieber/Stoller,
straddling black shellac like the King.

And what part of Brooklyn's Hispanic
growing-up pulse did Pomus/Shuman
not understand: to whose sideburned ear
did the flicked *go and have your fun* not
pander with its snapped-shut *don't forget
who's taking you home?*
              Then one of us heard
one of them, Doc or Mort, had lost the use
of both legs after some crazy war and had
his writing partner dance his mambo-loving
lovely wife, chaste – or soul-destroying –
every boardwalking, stars-above night.

Long after we'd witness interlocked names
whirl relentless in silver on a black label till
the stylus slithered centripetal over ungrooved
rink to the spindle.
                      Glowering jibe – or
awkward love? Either way team spirit wouldn't
survive 'Save the Last Dance''s charting.

CYCLOPS

Might once have figured you had
a sharp eye for the odd bright gem
alone by the wave-cleansed shore.
In your father's unpatented process
– back-shed lapidation driven
by a rewound spin-drier motor –
electricity accomplished in hours
those aeons of pre-Cambrian grind.

So you let them rub off one other
a while, then pick out the rarest,
perhaps one in a half-gross
(more, or less, than his ratio?)
to lie on significant papers
on your desk or bookshelf
till you find what he knew – that you
and all you know have enough,
that only receding tide gave them
that glister in paper-pale light.

Now try as you might to redeem
the discards, you just can't determine
if they've not worn down long enough
in your neo-palaeolithic tumble,
whether natural or lacquer is best,
or whether the years' fading shine
is blocking that one good eye.

SUMMER'S END

Begins languorously with a huzz
of flies over fish-heads in bins,
quickens in a home heavy
with plums left overnight in a bowl
when work took him away weeks ago,
gathers pace treading softly on peaches,
by a street-trader's barrow in August,
closes in as he sees himself sniff
cartons of newly bought milk.

He capitulates, lets it take over,
stores sugared black-banana
sandwiches until they putresce,
buys ling in the market to pick
fishscales from newspaper wrap,
keeps Port Salut higher and higher
until he can nail the obsession,
the olfactory indulgences lost
when the fifties passed on – that one day
heavy with light as Yankees
from Derry were beating a team
from a visiting warship the length
of a torpid, saturate, airless
Labor-Day Weekend afternoon,
when a naval-base seersucker mom
gave him a piercing-cold cola
in a thing like a bean-can with two
holes in top, from a fridge
in the back of a great tailgate Olds.

WRONG ABOUT LOVE

On the hide back-seat of another uncle's
'sixty-four Rover with armrest and setter-odour,
as we pass T. Sinclair Rainey's on Wellington Street
after the high-noon-long epic *How the West was Won,*
I mull Jimmy Stewart's porch-rocker old-saw
to the cowhand that's asked for his daughter
about its mattering more that he *liked* her, how
love might happen along a little later.

Now I think back on those screenwriters and actors
and the hosts of teachers and peddlers of well-spun advice
for growing boys, that would all have us believe
their dubious sagebrush verdicts on things of the heart,
and murmur a little sadly how wrong you can be;
and anyway it was probably *Shenandoah.*

LES AMANTS

In France they vote on Sunday.

In France you can go to mass
in the Protestant church and feel
you're siding with the underdog,
dreaming with the ancestors.

In France on a tepid night
you can still hear Nicholas
and Papa Bechet among *langoustes*
at Bofinger because it's still
deep, deep in the fifties there.

In France, on the Boul' Beaumarchais
you get carafes of ice-cold water
when your *glace* has chocolate sauce.

In France you can sleep in parks
as long as you don't upset
the Algerians and guitarists
who lived there first.

In France you wake to klaxons
of excited Citroën vans
and rings on a brass pole
that hang the floating nets
behind *jalousies* in a room
furnished out of a
Henry Miller novel and find
the woman you spent the night with

has left without trace to shop
at early *charcuteries* on Rue de Rivoli
for something lyonnaise or niçoise,
or for cous-cous, which you
haven't heard of, as it's still
the sixties and you've never
tasted aubergine.

In France you can play grown-up
and married with rings out of Woolworths
in Dover but the *patron* still registers
real names off your passports.

CALLING THE SHOTS

Times he walks out on the faculty, faking a migraine,
packs a bag, downtown on the jitney to book him a Greyhound
to a small border town where his woman's a teller in Second
National Finance, they meet at five on the steps,
go to her place where he fricassees chickpeas and rice,
and times if they're rich they'll drive over to Jackson's Hotel
where they both play the Wurlitzer, she chooses 'Send Me
    the Pillow',
come back through the frontier as orange spreads over the river,
and times they just sit, watch TV in the bar on the corner,
Colombo or *Kojak*, he's a beer, hers is vodka and lime,
eat steak and fries, talk of a future together,
and once in a while they head out to the place where
    his uncle's
the priest in Nuestra Señora, and join in the jive
to a small pull-out line-up of button-melodeon and fiddles
playing hot western-swing as if it was still 'fifty-six.

He breakfasts on shrimps, hard-boiled egg, Canadian whisky,
examines his stubble in what's left of the diner's bar-mirror,
calls the department, tells them he's still lying low
with the headache, another few days, maybe through to
    the weekend,
gets into a long-distance spat on the function of meaning,
thinks about having it both ways, then panics in case
she should start calling shots, walk out on her no-account
    husband.

CITY LOVE SONGS

Polis of nail-scissored green, Taiwan
electric-blue guitars with tremolo arm
hocked before Rogation Sunday and
the final catalogue payment, of pledged
nine-irons and bullworkers, tough brown
carry-out bags, *walk-ins welcome*
at 'The Head Gardeners', of white
lemonade and black taxis and
pay no more than 30 a score
on lit subway and tenement walls
where they'll sort lost ignition-keys
– continental models no bother –
out-of-any-hours, will have your SIM
unlocked and other services and off
before you've felt a mobile's absence;
city where the celebrated Niagaran
funambulist would walk his last wire;
seething locus of the spare-a-dime
paradigm, source of lethal dejections
and active contrition, of wall-
to-wall licensed grocers, eat-as-
much-as-you-like Heavenly Buffet
and Alec's Detox-ville Juice Bar,
shield each one of us (home
or away, straight and getting
straight, inside or out) *with thy
unceasing patronage* and forever
on account of her dress-rings
from earlier loves and the Gibson
Dobro mandolin we traded at

Joe Kavanagh's 'I-Buy-Anything'
(well before the incendiary
business) for a rough night-passage
to Heysham, *I will hold your people in*
the bleeding auricles and ventricles
of what passes, lately, for *my heart*.

THE NEW LIFE

For my first twenty-first, predating
the long abstention from flesh,
I sautéed non-vegetarian chops
with sweetcorn on the marital
electric frying-pan in Fulham.
                              When
we stumbled out of Jack Nicholson's
period gumshoe *Chinatown*,
shrugging Huston and Dunaway's
kill-to-keep secret, and hassled
through evening Gerrard Street throngs
– past ginger-root, bird's-nest –
we had scant appetite for exotic.

The eve of your twenty-second, after
my sesame'd fiery arrabbiata
and *vin-de-table* from the Superette,
you owned to a post-midnight compulsion
to re-eat.
                At ten-to-two, delving
off Fulham Broadway for 94-
night-bus-change with full hands
– monk's vegetables (Peking Palace),
Diwan-i-Am hot brinjal bhaji,
gherkins from Christoforou's van –
and ill-read in parenting lore,
it didn't click we were suddenly
adapting to new life. Not yet.

TOO MUCH REALITY

Sometime, in teasing out whether
bequeathing hostages to
posterity had been worldly wise
in that decade-long lacuna between
Soviet-Afghan and first Gulf Wars
in our sated westering democracies,
the cyclical death-cult lip-synched again
like hackneyed penny-dreadful fingerjoints
or the hirsute lady-traveller's ulna:

viz: fallen-off offers of buyable if
crudely duped videos wherein only
the *petites morts* were ersatz; one
band post-punk – not Metal but
some alloyed genre – advertising live
non-poultry Tuileries tableaux,
the Yard were – see broadsheets – *taking
an interest;* and for enough top dollar
to keep a rainforest clan per annum
one brave could be White City rabbit
in exec play-offs with added *schaden* . . .

whispers that tarnished those rearing
years, as our own *bildungs* clouded with
the intercostal blade and vanishing doughboy
when lights went up on the Mall, a
spavined, glimpsed hoof in a muffed slow-
foxtrot birl at some northern Locarno
(and again that holy year in the Auvergne,
Ardoyne, even Estremadura), then two

widowed dole-office brothers hacked off
and horribly done in in a Totteridge semi
locked from inside and the suspect beneficiary
verifiable elsewhere in Antwerp.

                              A ration
of rumours scotched when we repaired to
new realities, quiz-shows, shag-pile
bombing, monarchy, the coming down
and going up of walls, *still wars and
lechery*: aught else as ever holding fashion.

IMPEDIMENTA

Do not leave unattended.
                              Have by you
at all times the round-Ireland parental suitcase
you toted in turn through Earl's Court, gross
with Dylan LPs and wedding-gift toaster
first night of your honeymoon/exile,
straining biceps.
                              Keep watch on that tartan
duffel your stepmother stocked once a week
with Bonbel, Ben Shermans, ironed pyjamas,
as you cadged a lift to a fag-blown kip
in Damascus, Fitzroy or Ormeau.
                              Bear also
in mind the blue overnight that caught
the eye of a one-manned-Citybus driver
that knew you, ex-fireman-from-home,
as you fumbled to pay for the girl at your side
at the Myrtlefield bus-stop en route to an afterwards
breakfast in Marshall's on Donegall Square.
                              And
take care of the satchel your aunt won at hoopla
the August before you started Fairhill Street,
that you buckled with pride until Master O'Kane
trod on it, quashing lunch, a coffee-cake
segment inside that scented the leather
the remains of its embarrassed primary days.

Do not leave unattended.
                              Unwanted luggage
may be disposed of without further notice.

DO NOT WATCH THE ECLIPSE
OF THE SUN, MY LOVE

Our daughter's in Malaga phoning Wisconsin for tickets
to Jerez; our son and his girl are ploughing through fens
in trains with their backs to the engine, their faces to light
that is shading to argent then sable in parts of the city
as I, with the grey and no-longer-correcting Corona,
in my holt – between their superfluous rooms – light the last
of my pipes to jack-hammer letters on notepaper filched
out of bedrooms from Delhi to Eccles with every intent
of restoring, letters that tell you that soon you'll be back,
that I haven't once tuned the mandolin up since you sailed.

On the avenue neighbours are pouring out, pointing, stopping
each other from looking, with the whiff of illicit excitement
they tasted that midnight the van full of party-balloons
careened itself drunkardly, lurching from odd side to even,
compacting impartially Alfas and Zetecs, encouraging
un-nodding acquaintance *déshabillé*'d onto the street.

While you, between our two towns in your static Fiesta,
– between stolen mountain and vanishing lake –
admit to your being amazed that what's almost occluded
is much more intense than what stares you fair in the face:
and I give you this sliver, this shivering shred of unwelcome
advice, my love – do not watch the eclipse of the sun.

BEDSIT

for Ruth, on her sixteenth birthday

Not quite the way we saw it, style
we had in mind. Like where's the oak-
framed oval mirror? Beige-ish tiles
that came unstuck? And who said you could chuck
the desiccated purple weeds and vase
or hide the photo-montage of the dolls'
tea-party, gouached moon-man? As
for painting black the Ashleyed walls
and Oxfamming the duvet, watered silk,
it must have cost – sure I get the art
with all the techno bits, the tube-black desk,
PC, card-index, Walkman, body-parts
cropped from *NME* or *Sky* or *Face*:
well nineties, I concede – and just as mixed
on eighties features, deep blue glass
collection, gothic iron candlesticks
and beeswax candles: but what goes on,
with sixties retro-chic, that cotton throw?
And hanging from the window-hasp, your *pièce
de résistance*, the tights, Sahara Tan,
hand-basin-rinsed, but don't you think a little
L-Shaped Room? Too *Wednesday Play* by far?
OK, it's your room – who am I to quibble?
I only knocked to ask, as it's May now
and nights are lighter, whether you'll still
want your tartan-clad hot-water bottle filled?

DANDELION CLOCK

If once in the runnels of years
in a silver light something like this,
on catching a *soupçon* of glance
that might have disproved you can't
ever know what the person
closest to you really feels,
if he'd woven, at that very point
in the fractions that make up a life,
a tentative net of abstractions
to fling at the exiting moment,
at the light illusory flittering
schmetterling of oncelongago
as it quivered above, behind,
out of range of their hesitant gaze
and out through a sliver of sun
between curtains on anodised rails
they'd have bought at a paintshop in Redcar –
perhaps then he'd have known for sure.

SOUTH

She took him places he'd not dreamed,
had known since a child; threw him
keys to keep the shooting brake ticking
over as she went for punts on a lashing
early-closing day in Clones – a funeral
crossing the square – took him swimming
off Ventry strand where only Skelligs,
Blaskets, Patagonia . . .
lay between them and Valparaíso.

Drove him down unmetalled roads
to Cistercian sites, ruins of big,
fictional houses. He panned her tapes
for R & B and early tangos,
the lament Jim sang to Nora,
told her how in a family of ten –
including an aged step-aunt – they'd filled
every packed road-mile from 'The West's Awake'
to 'A, You're Adorable' and 'I Don't See Me'
while he'd navigated, co-ordinated picnics.

Once, he took the wheel and she was
deep beside him under a jacket
seeking out last night's lost rest:
started awake as he drew up
at lights, spotted a corner hoarding.
'Mullingar,' she whispered, though she'd only
seen it once in a lifetime before,
then 'Evergreen . . .' – before drifting off
as the lights changed – inexplicably
unyielding later to hours of talk.

And once in a broad, unhurried street
when she pinpointed a second-floor sash
he could see a ribboned child look down
– on headscarves of 1962,
some horseshoed, some with Lourdes –
on boys in first communion suits
and men in berets, hats or caps,
with rhubarb in bicycle-baskets –
and behind, her young father in soft shirtsleeves
telling her not to lean against the glass.

NOT BUYING A DOG

Now two dogs later they motor
on cart ruts between foxglove ditches
in a clunkily ill-tempered shooting brake,
passing, in clearings, auberges
and hostelries glad with awnings,
names he translates: *The Gosling,*
The Case Is Altered – this one
he insists goes back to the
Thirty Years War – then *Sugar Loaves,*
Land of Liberty, Peace and Plenty.

Now it is easy. That time
they'd snuck, for a very first jaunt,
out of immigrant streets on the mauve
un-reupholstered rolling-stock
of the overground suburban Metro,
had come to an unmanned platform
in hills to the west of the river
where no one spoke vaguely like them
and with only light hints of there having
been a taxi once before Munich.

That time they had stopped at the inn
of a Bergamasc exile who grilled them
a freshwater sturgeon and she,
great with child, had fled from the gaze
of the dish's pale eyes on its bedding of
partly boiled chard, to wait,
exhausted, by parallel lines,

for the train to the city and home,
convincing each other the dog-ranch
would not lightly elude them again.

GETTING STARTED

The digital display reads 09:01,
campanile clock five-to,
on Founder's Block of Benton Graduate School;

the percolator's not yet hot; necessary
fix is strong by ten,
first milestone in an uneventful day.

Crazy, of course, but after years of punching
Dalton-Seimnitz series through
a number-crunching, parallel computer,

I lived my life along such lines,
assured I could find
the perfect algorithm to generate

or decompose in seconds any code –
not that I expected
reward, just recognition in the field.

But word had filtered out: I deciphered
panic in the tense young men
who cleared my desk of theses, files and tapes . . .

the Babbage Museum of Numeracy, I can see,
could be quite a challenge,
my first acquisition a nineteen forty-one

code-breaking computator to arrive
in three months' time.
Till then I've little else to do.

The colon flashes on the digital display:
my desk is cleared for action:
09:05. The clock has yet to strike.

ISLAND

Maybe this sunset that postboxy gloss
on a sun-hardened sash-window's jamb,
those worked-iron coathooks, cool earth of the tiles
on the floor of this lost-island café
                                        'll be some of the shots
in our *Nouvelle Vague* fishing-port tryst.
                                        Then
by the blue Oldsmobile on the car-ferry's deck
we'll dream of the home we acquire, north of the sound,
where we fix the verandah, paint nursery windows
and you make new friends, and their kids meet ours –
again and again in our own basement screenings
that flick to the point Falconetti rides up
with his Vespa
                        the ivory phone rings too loud
in an ivy-clad porch
                                    some real-estate deal
keeps me later in town, and you, the circle
lets into secrets with talk of a new tennis coach.

ET IN ARCADIA

Lake Balaton, May 2002

Remembering only never
being with her in haygrass,
burrs on the rug they would use
for the fatal dog's last journey,
in that made-for-TV with a Fair Isle
woodwork-master and the prow
of a White Star dividing clover
and safe ewes;
                  never looking
out over broom and wild
rhubarb onto the sail-infested
Aegean looking-glass, car-keys
in her strawberry smock pocket,
two-way bus-company ticket in his;

never knowing lapping as sibilant,
hushed, as on this manicured shore
of a landlocked Hungarian sea
unbounded as far as the eye
ahead, but offering the voyager
– once past the *mezzo camino* –
illimitable vistas behind.

PAVLOVA'S DOGS

In the three-ringed circus of memory
he knew how the crash of the hi-hat
at the start of the 'Galop' from *Orpheus*
was the cue for the waistcoated tumblers
and cowgirls to whip back the flaps
while Fanfandel shooed out the dappled
grey steed with the pooch on its saddle;
the balance depended on terror,
as sure as his own hands were glued
to the car's steering wheel on this second
or third lap of the Savoy Circus ring.

But the secret as yet undivined
was whether the terrified yelp
told the Shetland to exit the ring
before the dog lost its nerve and absconded
or whether the final crescendo
was the cue for the pony; or whether
the well-drilled saxophonists watched
for the poodle to give them the nod.

In either case, driving to Wagner
on a radio blind to his signals,
he had several circuits to go.

SWOOPING

Today while you were out
I buzzed the house in passing
in a twin-prop DC-9.

I mean, I hadn't meant to
but after several plastic
cups of in-flight Riesling

when we began descending
I sauntered to the cockpit.
Apparently they're quite

unflapped by such requests,
it's just a small diversion,
just a straying from the flight-path.

Anyway, the back-roof,
the one we're always slating,
looks OK from up above

and the ghastly red-brick gothic
of St Alban's in the park
would almost pass for pretty,

like when I had that model
in the attic with the houses
and the movies and the factories

in a scene from nineteen fifty
and the tiny plastic milk-float
that came by post from Hamleys.

It's not like the Snake Pass
where you bank and soar with condors –
make believe you're in the Andes

with the little mountain tarns
set like mirrors in the papier-
mâché ochre hillscape –

but I guess it's hard to beat
the buzz you get from swooping
on the neighbours in the evening

or watching Stanley frantic
in the garden at the back –
and when I crawled the fuselage

I could have put my hand out
and touched the fascia boarding
of the house next-door-but-one.

IN A COLD CLIMATE

Ten times as deep as in its unaltered form,
the Inuit have names for fifty-something kinds of it.

The Iroquois have fewer and more rare,
translated here for tongues like ours that must
twist epithets around the melting noun –
that which seems to be but is not; which
is but alters to the touch and flows
away; that blurs the view but does not lie;
hard cutting hails that lash at sails and spars
and radar, make orphans of whole class
photographs; featureless lands of it that lock-
in survey ships for decades at a time;
great silent drifts that isolate entire worlds;
stuff that from its falling till its thaw
sees out a cycle of the seasons and whose
leaving carries copses, houses, sheep
and kine, in rivers down to seas of tears.

And stuff we thought was lost, bright suddenness
falling through a faded day – beside
the synagogue in Oranienburgstrasse,
its permaguard of armoured cars – as we,
eleven days together on the road,
sip anisette and watch that slow descent
in *flakes* again, *as large and light as maple leaves.*

AFRICAN QUEEN

I

September, early, our river
a torpid ditch where herons
gangle – gawky, will-less –
on a 1929 houseboat
out of Rotterdam, its deck's-worth
of algae-ified plastic *gerania*
fading to white amid ductwork
and keels that no longer lift,
freighted with Sainsbury's trolleys
and remaindered patio sets,
tarred with a mildly sulphurous
primordial mulligatawny –
and here a metal-hull launch,
tender to Hanseatic gunships,
now holed below decks: the mechanical
museum admits no trippers,
the player-less Bremen-town-band
as dead as the chess-playing Turk,
the calliope with cracked waxen rolls.

II

Now fast-moving water
snatches osier and willow fistfuls,
peacocks screech, cockatiels
flit in and out of the barn where
the late martyr spent his last orisons . . .
Rare breeds, De-Cuyp-like cattle,
low in the butterfly meadow and pubs
flare carnivalesque along

the swelling bank. Outside
The Apprentice, where we took the kids
after work, a miracle in varnish
and brass used in that forties film
hoots past to the eyot. What
changed? Just a quotidian
tide-turn? Your voice-mail
on the mobile – *Guess you're*
on the river. Ring later. Love?

OUT OF TOUCH, MY BABY

As dated, say, as playing-cards
or stripping pine, the London bus,
paper lanterns, Mothercare,
beansprouts, cottage cheese, Ryvita,
Welfare State, Poll Tax and us;

as out-of-time as folk and jazzmen,
poems & pints, as herbal tea,
bass saxophones, Moog synthesisers,
slide guitar and Ian Dury,
Capital, the GLC;

as retrograde as sci-fi plots,
moon-walking, Skylab, Steeleye Span,
Green Lantern and the caped crusader,
sandwich makers, microwavers,
Lea and Perrins, frying pans;

as little-thought-of now as Oxfam,
post-war clinics, Wedgwood Benn,
as Co-op stamps or saving mammals,
golden eagles, Tepee Valley,
denim dungarees on men;

as *démodé* as care or action,
community, the people, God,
as *then* as teenage, gifted, young,
Ted Kennedy and Mao Tse-tung,
as dead as words like Taig and Protestant;

as out-of-date as, maybe, faith,
a silver thorn, a bloody rose,
as so un-here-and-now as hope
in real tomorrows for our kids,
while there's still life, while blood still flows;

as dated as this thing between us
people make like they're ashamed of,
ardent, hard as stone, that alters
when it altercation finds,
the thing I hardly dare to name, love.

BOARDING-HOUSE BOOKCASE

Wakened to that hexagonal West Country light
inscaping by vicarage B & B shutters,
I touch your shoulder strap, think back on the face

of a husband called Cathal hung on the tenacity
of badgers in a paperback Irish short stories
you gave me the night I would spend on my own

at the top of the Commercial Hotel in Strabane
before thumbing my way back by Sion, Dungannon,
flicking leaves of a life that altered me, much

as the one – I was ten – of *Bous Stephanoumenos,*
the pale little boy with the ache in his breadbasket
he got from fellows that pushed him face-down

in a ditch, but you knew the hurting was really
because of an aunt with the two velvet brushes,
for the lover that no one could speak of,

a tale that had gnawed inside one long night in Falcarragh –
that had gone in the morning, leaving me: Chesterton,
Macken, O'Flaherty, Birmingham, Wodehouse and Tey.

NOLI-ME-TANGERE

Always on the head at the strand's
reach, a keep, or remnants of the lavabo
of a dissolute monastery and always
within or behind, the detritus
of spent hopes, cartons and crisp
packets: and ever as you depart,
a flower so small, so fine, so odd
in its star-like leaves or petal-shaped
stamen you not only know it cannot
exist in any other part of the world
and that it is surely nameless, innocent
of taxonomy, but that this,
slipped now as love-offering for later
with covert elation in that shirt-pocket,
is, at least until the wash, the only
one of its kind in existence.

OLD WINTER'S SONG

In windswept public canyons
of a Les Halles Sunday a street-
couple – violin & musette, she
must be in her seventies and
would remember the film –
gasp a purposed slow-foxtrot
through Jacques Prévert's song
. . . *le vent du nord les emporte*
dans la nuit froide de l'oubli . . .
you played from the pale
blue song-sheet before you drove
us to New Row in Coleraine
for Trinity College Grade One.

Alice Smylie who came in at
dinner-hour, days you wouldn't
be there – exams or hospital –
swore it must be some radio
station. Years till I would grasp
the harmonic minor blowing
west across a continent to Paris
like the wind of forgetfulness,
would notice the English
euphemisms for *mortes, la*
vie sépare . . . But the sweeping
out of sight still echoes.

Tu vois, je n'ai pas oublié
la chanson que tu me chantais.

ACKNOWLEDGEMENTS

Acknowledgement is due to the following for first publication: *Poetry Ireland, Times Literary Supplement, Honest Ulsterman, Poetry London, Magma, Wolf, Fortnight, Southfield, Upstart!, Cimarron Review* (US), *Pivot* (US) and The Poetry Workshop website (www.carpenter.btinternet.co.uk/hpwp). 'Carrick-a-Rede Rope Bridge' appeared in the Louis MacNeice centenary publication *My Mother Wore a Yellow Dress* (Carrickfergus Borough Council and Arts Council of Northern Ireland, 2008), and 'So Many Revolutions Per Minute' was first published in *Divers: The Poetry Workshop Anthology* (Aark Arts, 2008). 'Love on a Rock' won first prize in the Strokestown International Poetry Competition (2006). 'Do Not Watch the Eclipse of the Sun, My Love' was awarded second prize in the Amnesty International Poetry Competition (2002). 'City Love Songs', 'Summer's End', 'Difference', 'Careless Talk', 'Bedsit', 'Island' and 'In a Cold Climate' have been awarded prizes in Kent and Sussex, Bridport International, Amnesty International and London Writers poetry competitions.